A Celebration
of Christmas

Christmas is more than a day or a season; it's the foundation stone of our hope in human goodness and generosity. It's a time of celebrating the best in all of us. And it's a time of acknowledging that it all began when God gave us His best in the form of a tiny babe in a hay-filled crèche. In the pages of this little book, we have included the essence of Christmas—the story of that first incredible gift, the Christ child. We've also provided a sampling of the simple joys of the season—carols, games, stories, recipes, verse, and inspirational quotes. We hope that *A Celebration of Christmas* will make you want to shout: "Peace on earth, goodwill toward men!"

The Christmas Story

LUKE 2:1-20 NKJV

And it came to pass in those days that a decree went out for Caesar Augustus that all the world should be registered. This census first took place while Quirinius was governing Syria. So all went to be registered, everyone to his own city.

Joseph also went up from Galilee, out of the city of Nazareth, into Judea, to the city of David, which is called Bethlehem, because he was of the house and lineage of David, to be registered with Mary, his betrothed wife, who was with child. So it was, that while they were there, the days were completed for her to be delivered. And she brought forth her firstborn Son, and wrapped Him in swaddling cloths, and laid Him in a manger, because there was no room for them in the inn.

Now there were in the same country shepherds living out in the fields, keeping watch over their flock by night. And behold, an angel of the Lord stood before them, and they were greatly afraid. Then the angel said to them, "Do not be afraid, for behold, I bring you good tidings of great joy which will be to all people. For there is born to you this day in the city of David a Savior, who is Christ the Lord. And this will be the sign to you: You will find a Babe wrapped in swaddling cloths, lying in a manger."

And suddenly there was with the angel a multitude of the heavenly host praising God and saying: "Glory to God in the highest, And on earth peace, goodwill toward men!"

So it was, when the angels had gone away from them into heaven that the shepherds said to one another, "Let us now go to Bethlehem and see this thing that has come to pass, which the Lord has made known to us." And they came with haste and found Mary and Joseph, and the Babe lying in a manger.

Now when they had seen Him, they made widely known the saying, which was told them by the shepherds. But Mary kept all these things and pondered them in her heart. Then the shepherds returned, glorifying and praising God for all the things that they had heard and seen, as it was told them.

When we celebrate Christmas we are celebrating
that amazing time when the Word that shouted
all the galaxies into being, limited all power, and for love of us
came to us in the powerless body of a human baby.

MADELINE L'ENGLE

Paper Sack Christmas

BY ELECE HOLLIS

Everyone was poor in Oklahoma in 1933, but most were not accustomed to poverty. It had jumped them from behind like a snarling cat on an unsuspecting prey, tearing apart families, homes and dreams. Grandpop's family made out better than most because he owned a small neighborhood grocery store. In the now non-existent town of Tribbey, Oklahoma, Grandpop's store served as gas station, post office, grocery, and general meeting place.

At his wooden counter, a roller of brown wrapping paper and a string dispenser resided beside an ornate cash register and a porcelain grocer's scale.

The register had long since grown silent. The cash drawer sat open, no cash changed hands. To be sure, Grandpop couldn't stock the store as well as he'd been able to before the crash. But, people still had to eat, and they had need of sewing needles and spools of thread, besides the basics: flour, sugar, beans, kerosene and coffee. Normally, folks grew their own garden vegetables, but the drought had put an end to that. Even raising chickens and hunting and fishing became non-productive as the dust bowl settled down over the state, smothering hope.

Grandpop gave credit and vowed he would continue as long as he could get anything to sell, and as long as he could feed his own family. There were canned goods gathering dust on the shelves behind the counter. Dill pickles languished in brine barrels. Peppermints, lemon drops, and horehound candies slowly crystallized in bell jars. Bolts of cloth mellowed on the exposed rolled edges that faced out into the store. Light from the two front windows and four bare bulbs hanging suspended from white ceramic fixtures had faded them.

The depression had faded Grandpop too. It aged him. It hurt him to see children hungry and ragged. It pained him to watch friends and neighbors lose their farms. So Grandpop gave credit in a time when it made no sense to give credit, when chances of recouping his losses were surely non-existent. Grandpop trusted people and very few took his trust lightly.

It grieved Grandpop that many folks would not accept help no matter how terribly their children needed things. He liked to give penny candy to the children who came into his store. He especially hurt for those wearing hungry faces that seemed to cry out for something sweet. Those children would shake their heads and say staunchly, "We don't take charity, Mr. Michael." Finally, one Christmas as Grandpop contemplated the pain of watching children pass the holidays without a visit from Santa Claus or even a peppermint stick in their stockings, he came up with a plan. If every child in town were presented with a treat, then no one could define the treats as "charity."

So Grandpop went to work. He rounded up the languishing bags of candy no one could afford to buy, and ordered in extra fruit and a big bag of nuts. The whole family joined in the task of filling the brown paper lunch bags. On the night of the school Christmas program, Santa (Grandma, dressed in a red suit and a huge black belt and sporting a cotton beard) bustled to the front of the overcrowded classroom and passed a bag to every person present. Grandpop was thrilled. He had gotten in a lick on those bullies—Poverty and Pride. He had spread some happiness in the midst of the harsh times. It's possible he enjoyed it more than the hungriest kid there!

Now in many rural Oklahoma towns, the tradition of the paper sacks at Christmas is still alive and well. Even in our prosperous times when children eat sweets daily and an orange is not even considered a treat, the tradition has lingered, paying tribute to those sturdy survivors who refused to let the Great Depression rob them of their Christmas joy.

Here's to the day of good will, cold weather, and warm hearts.

CHRISTMAS FUN

Reindeer Droppings

VARIETY OF CHOCOLATE CANDY BARS

PAPER PLATES

SIGNS WITH REINDEER NAMES
(Dasher, Dancer, Prancer, Vixen, etc.)—one for each variety of chocolate bar

PAPER AND PENCILS FOR EACH PLAYER

Crush pieces of candy to form clumps (reindeer droppings) and put them on small paper plates. Place a sign with a reindeer's name on it beside each plate. (Don't forget to make an answer key!) Players are to study the plates of "reindeer droppings" and identify what type of candy is on each plate. Have the players write down their answers along with the reindeer name of each specimen. Read the answers and award a prize to the one(s) who guessed the most correctly.

CHRISTMAS GOODIES

Cheesy Christmas Tree

1 (8 OZ.) PACKAGE EXTRA SHARP CHEDDAR CHEESE, SHREDDED

1 (8 OZ.) PACKAGE MEDIUM CHEDDAR CHEESE, SHREDDED

1/2 CUP GRATED ONION

1/2 CUP MAYONNAISE

1/2 TSP RED PEPPER

1 CUP CHOPPED FRESH PARSLEY

FRESH CRANBERRIES

Combine the first 5 ingredients, and mix well.
Shape into a cone and cover with the parsley.
Place cranberries on the tree as ornaments.

CHRISTMAS CAROL

Deck the Halls!

Deck the halls with boughs of holly,

Fa la la la la, la la la la.

Tis the season to be jolly,

Fa la la la la, la la la la.

Don we now our gay apparel,

Fa la la, la la la, la la la.

Troll the ancient Yuletide carol,

Fa la la la la, la la la la.

See the blazing Yule before us,

Fa la la la la, la la la la.

Strike the harp and join the chorus.

Fa la la la la, la la la la.

Follow me in merry measure,

Fa la la, la la la, la la la.

While I tell of Yuletide treasure,
Fa la la la la, la la la la.
Fast away the old year passes,
Fa la la la la, la la la la.
Hail the new, ye lads and lasses,
Fa la la la la, la la la la.
Sing we joyous, all together,
Fa la la, la la la, la la la.
Heedless of the wind and weather,
Fa la la la la, la la la la.

The Christmas favorite "Deck the Halls" is thought to be Welch—the music at least—deriving from a sixteenth century folk tune called, "Nos Galan." Mozart composed a piano and violin duet around it in the eighteenth century. The lyrics, however, are believed to be American. No one knows who wrote them, only that the music and lyrics were first recorded in 1881.

Here We Come A-Wassailing

Here we come a-wassailing among the leaves so green;

Here we come a-wandering, so fair to be seen.

Love and joy come to you, and to you our wassail, too.

And God bless you and send you a Happy New Year

And God bless you and send you a Happy New Year

We are not daily beggars that beg from door to door;

But we are neighbors' children whom you have seen before.

Refrain

We have a little purse made of ratching leather skin;

We want a little sixpence to line it well within.

Refrain

God bless the master of this house, likewise the mistress, too;

And all the little children that round the table go.

Refrain

This Christmas favorite celebrates the New Year. Wassail today is typically heated cider or tea spiced with cinnamon and nutmeg. Traditionally, residents would invite carolers inside for a cup of wassail to warm them before continuing their journey through the neighborhood singing and spreading holiday cheer.

Ave Maria

Ave Maria! Maiden mild.
Ah! Listen to a maiden's prayer;
For Thou canst hear amid the wild,
'Tis Thou, 'tis Thou canst save amid
despair.

We slumber safely till the morrow,
'Tho e'en by men outcast, revil'd.
Oh maiden, see a maiden's sorrow,
Oh Mother, hear a suppliant child!
Ave Maria!

Ave Maria! Undefil'd!
The flinty couch where on we're sleeping
Shall seem with down of elder pil'd,
If Thou above sweet watch art keeping,

The murky cavern's air so heavy
Shall breathe of balm, if Thou hast
smil'd;
O Maiden hear, a maiden's pleading,
O Mother, hear a suppliant child!
Ave Maria!

Ave Maria! Stainless styl'd!
Each fiend of air of earthly essence,
From this their wonted haunt exil'd,
Shall flee before Thy holy presence!

We bow, beneath our cares o'reladen,
To Thy dear guidance reconcil'd;
Then hear, oh Maid, a simple maiden
And for a father hear a child!
Ave Maria!

The much-loved Ave Maria prayer has been used in personal and public devotions for centuries. The first part of the song is taken from Scripture—Luke 1:28, 42.

It has been put to music many times, but one of the most impressive and well-known is Franz Schubert's lovely composition. Schubert wrote his wonderful musical interpretation, now associated with the Ave Maria while on holiday in Upper Austria in 1838. He originally set his music to a poem by Sir Walter Scott rather than the beautiful prayer we are familiar with today.

CHRISTMAS CAROL

O Christmas Tree!

O Christmas tree, O Christmas tree!
How are thy leaves so verdant!
O Christmas tree, O Christmas tree,
How are thy leaves so verdant!

Not only in the summertime,
But even in winter is thy prime.
O Christmas tree, O Christmas tree,
How are thy leaves so verdant!

O Christmas tree, O Christmas tree,
Much pleasure doth thou bring me!
O Christmas tree, O Christmas tree,
Much pleasure doth thou bring me!

For every year the Christmas tree,
Brings to us all both joy and glee.
O Christmas tree, O Christmas tree,
Much pleasure doth thou bring me!

> O Christmas tree, O Christmas tree,
> Thy candles shine out brightly!
> O Christmas tree, O Christmas tree,
> Thy candles shine out brightly!

Each bough doth hold its tiny light,
That makes each toy to sparkle bright.
O Christmas tree, O Christmas tree,
Thy candles shine out brightly!

"O Christmas Tree" is a traditional carol of German origin. The author of the lyrics and the music are both unknown. But there is no mistaking this little carol's popularity through the years. The melody has been used as the state song for four states—Iowa, Maryland, Michigan, and New Jersey.

CHRISTMAS CAROL

Patapan

William, beat your drum with joy!
Sound your fife now, Robin boy!
While your instruments you play,
Tu-re lu-re-lu, pata patapan.
While your instruments you play,
We shall sing Noel so gay.

People in the days of yore
Did the King of Kings adore;
While your instruments you play,
Tu-re lu-re-lu, pata patapan.
While your instruments you play,
We must do the same today.

Like mankind and mankind's Lord
Fife and drum are in accord;
While your instruments you play,
Tu-re lu-re-lu, pata patapan.
While your instruments you play,
Let us dance and sing today.

"Patapan" was written around 1700. The melody was probably borrowed from a popular folk song of that time, while the words are thought to be a somewhat more versatile predecessor to the popular carol, "The Little Drummer Boy." Bernard de la Monnoye, a talented carol writer from the Burgundy region of France, is credited with writing the lyrics.

A Little Snow Bird

BY KATE DOUGLAS WIGGIN
AN EXCERPT FROM *THE BIRDS' CHRISTMAS CAROL*

It was very early Christmas morning, and in the stillness of the dawn, with the soft snow falling on the housetops, a little child was born in the Bird household.

They had intended to name the baby Lucy, if it were a girl; but they hadn't expected her on Christmas morning, and a real Christmas baby was not to be lightly named—the whole family agreed in that.

They were consulting about it in the nursery. Mr. Bird said that he had assisted in naming the three boys, and that he should leave this matter entirely to Mrs. Bird; Donald wanted the child called "Maud," after a pretty little curly-haired girl who sat next him in school; Paul chose "Luella," for Luella was the nurse who had been with him during his whole babyhood, up to the time of his first trousers, and the name suggested all sorts of comfortable things. Uncle Jack said that the first girl should always be named for her mother, no matter how hideous the name happened to be.

Grandma said that she would prefer not to take any part in the discussion, and everybody suddenly remembered that Mrs. Bird had thought of naming the baby Lucy, for Grandma herself; and, while it would be indelicate for her to favor that name, it would be against human nature for her to suggest any other, under the circumstances.

Hugh, the "hitherto baby," if that is a possible term, sat in one corner and said nothing, but felt, in some mysterious way, that his nose was out of joint; for there was a newer baby now, a possibility he had never taken into consideration; and the "first girl," too, a still higher development of treason, which made him actually green with jealousy.

But it was too profound a subject to be settled then and there, on the spot; besides, Mama had not been asked, and everybody felt it rather absurd, after all, to forestall a decree that was certain to be absolutely wise, just and perfect.

The reason that the subject had been brought up at all so early in the day lay in the fact that Mrs. Bird never allowed her babies to go over night unnamed. She was a person of so great decision of character that she would have blushed at such a thing; she said that to let blessed babies go dangling and dawdling about without names, for months and months, was enough to ruin them for life. She also said that if one could not make up one's mind in twenty-four hours, it was a sign that—but I will not repeat the rest, as it might prejudice you against the most charming woman in the world.

So, Donald took his new velocipede and went out to ride up and down the stone pavement and notch the shins of innocent people as they passed by, while Paul spun his musical top on the front steps.

But Hugh refused to leave the scene of action. He seated himself on the top stair in the hall, banged his head against the railing a few times, just by way of uncorking the vials of his wrath, and then subsided into gloomy silence, waiting to declare war if more "first girl babies" were thrust upon a family already surfeited with that unnecessary article.

Meanwhile, dear Mrs. Bird lay in her room, weak, but safe and happy with her sweet girl baby by her side and the heaven of motherhood opening before her. Nurse was making gruel in the kitchen, and the room was dim and quiet. There was a cheerful open fire in the grate, but though the shutters were closed, the side windows that looked out on the Church of our Saviour, next door, were wide open.

Suddenly a sound of music poured out into the bright air and drifted into the chamber. It was the boy-choir singing Christmas anthems. Higher and higher rose the clear, fresh voices,

21

full of hope and cheer, as children's voices always are. Fuller and fuller grew the burst of melody as one glad strain fell upon another in joyful harmony:

"Carol, brothers, carol,
Carol joyfully,
Carol the good tidings,
Carol merrily!
"And pray a gladsome Christmas
For all your fellow-men:
Carol, brothers, carol,
Christmas Day again."

Mrs. Bird thought, as the music floated in upon her gentle sleep, that she had slipped into heaven with her new baby, and that the angels were bidding them welcome. But the tiny bundle by her side stirred a little, and though it was scarcely more than the ruffling of a feather, she awoke; for the mother-ear is so close to the heart that it can hear the faintest whisper of a child.

She opened her eyes and drew the baby closer. It looked like a rose dipped in milk, she thought, this pink and white blossom of girlhood, or like a pink cherub, with its halo of pale yellow hair, finer than floss silk.

"Why, my baby," whispered Mrs. Bird in soft surprise, "I had forgotten what day it was. You are a little Christmas child, and we will name you 'Carol'—mother's little Christmas Carol!"

"What!" said Mr. Bird, coming in softly and closing the door behind him.

"Why, Donald, don't you think 'Carol' is a sweet name for a Christmas baby? It came to me just a moment ago in the singing as I was lying here half asleep and half awake."

"I think it is a charming name, dear heart, and that it sounds just like you, and I hope that,

22

being a girl, this baby has some chance of being as lovely as her mother," at which speech from the baby's papa, Mrs. Bird, though she was as weak and tired as she could be, blushed with happiness. And so Carol came by her name.

Of course, it was thought foolish by many people, though Uncle Jack declared laughingly that it was very strange if a whole family of Birds could not be indulged in a single Carol; and Grandma, who adored the child, thought the name much more appropriate than Lucy, but was glad that people would probably think it short for Caroline.

Perhaps because she was born in holiday time, Carol was a very happy baby. Of course, she was too tiny to understand the joy of Christmas-tide, but people say there is everything in a good beginning, and she may have breathed-in unconsciously the fragrance of evergreens and holiday dinners; while the peals of sleigh-bells and the laughter of happy children may have fallen upon her baby ears and wakened in them a glad surprise at the merry world she had come to live in.

Her cheeks and lips were as red as holly berries; her hair was for all the world the color of a Christmas candle-flame; her eyes were bright as stars; her laugh like a chime of Christmas bells, and her tiny hands forever outstretched in giving.

Such a generous little creature you never saw! A spoonful of bread and milk had always to be taken by Mama or nurse before Carol could enjoy her supper; and whatever bit of cake or sweetmeat found its way into her pretty fingers, it was straightway broken in half and shared with Donald, Paul or Hugh; and, when they made believe nibble the morsel with affected enjoyment, she would clap her hands and crow with delight.

"Why does she do it?" asked Donald, thoughtfully; "None of us boys ever did."

"I hardly know," said Mama, catching her darling to her heart, "except that she is a little Christmas child, and so she has a tiny share of the blessedest birthday the world ever saw!"

23

From home to home and heart to heart,
from one place to another.
The warmth and joy of Christmas
brings us closer to each other.

AUTHOR UNKNOWN